FREE M

A Play in Two Acts
by
CHARLES SMITH

Recipient of the 2004 Joseph Jefferson Award for
Outstanding New Work in Chicago

Dramatic Publishing
Woodstock, Illinois • England • Australia • New Zealand

IMPORTANT BILLING AND CREDIT REQUIREMENTS

All producers of the play *must* give credit to the Author of the play in all programs distributed in connection with performances of the play and in all instances in which the title of the play appears for purposes of advertising, publicizing or otherwise exploiting the play and/or a production. The name of the Author *must* also appear on a separate line, on which no other name appears, immediately following the title, and *must* appear in size of type not less than fifty percent the size of the title type. Biographical information on the Author, if included in the playbook, may be used in all programs. *In all programs these notices must appear:*

"Produced by special arrangement with
THE DRAMATIC PUBLISHING COMPANY of Woodstock, Illinois"

and

"Originally produced at Victory Gardens Theater, Chicago, Ill.,
Dennis Zacek, artistic director and production director,
January 2004."

The paradox of education is precisely this—that as one begins to become conscious one begins to examine the society in which he is being educated.

— *James Baldwin*

SPECIAL THANKS

While ultimately, it is my hope that *Free Man of Color* is a play about three people whose lives intersected at one point in time, it is also a play that touches on other topics including the Presbyterians in Ohio in the early 1800s, the American Colonization Society, the founding of Ohio University and the history of Liberia, all topics about which I knew nothing before beginning this project. While I am certain to unintentionally fail to include some who helped me, I would like to thank George Bain and the staff of the Ohio University Alden Library Archives, Scott Carson, Lisa Carson, Robert Glidden, Betty Hollow, Najee Muhammad, Connie Perdreau, Rusty Smith, Lorraine Wochna, the School of Theater at Ohio University, members of the Playwrights Workshop at Ohio University, and my wife, Lisa Quinn, for the generosity of their time, talent and wisdom.

AUTHOR'S NOTE

Free Man of Color is about John Newton Templeton, the first black man to attend Ohio University. The play is set between the years 1824 and 1828, four decades before Abraham Lincoln signed the emancipation proclamation. During that time, proslavery factions argued against emancipation by arguing that blacks were merely children that needed to be cared for. They argued that even blacks who appeared to be self-sufficient, smart and educated were not smart or educated at all. They argued that blacks who appeared to be intelligent were merely imitating whites. This same argument was later used by segregationists to support their continued call for separate schools in this country.

Today, two hundred years later, these inflammatory accusations still abound. However, the source of these accusations today is not proslavery advocates or even staunch segregationists. According to scores of politicians, social commentators and pundits, the source of these demeaning accusations are African- American children themselves. Politicians, social commentators, pundits, and even a few rich black celebrities claim that today's African-American students are hostile toward education. They claim that the few African-American students who excel in scholastic achievement are teased by their peers. They claim that these students are attacked, ridiculed and accused by other African-American students of "acting white."

If this is true, the implications are horrifying. If true, the racists have reached nirvana; they no longer have to spend time devising ways to police Negroes to keep them in their place, the Negro children have been trained to police themselves. But I suspect something else is happening here.

There is a difference between education and indoctrination. Education is teaching a student *how* to think. Indoctrination is teaching a student *what* to think. The premise of education—real education—is that a student should be given the tools and the means by which to conduct his own intellectual inquiry. The conclusion of that inquiry should be the student's and student's alone. When a student develops his or her own ideas, ideas that may be different than those espoused by textbooks, that student should be feted. But far too many times, students today are censured and their ideas depreciated. And our children are smart; they know what's going on. Give them a few rudimentary tools and they develop their own ideas. They know what they think and they know what's in their hearts. They also know what the (usually white) authority figure standing in front of them wants them to say. Some do what is asked of them and mindlessly repeat the party line. Some refuse to parrot the party line, then ridicule those who do. Many of these students are destroyed. Only a few are lucky enough to have experienced teachers who fully support the development of the individual mind and spirit.

In *Free Man of Color*, John Newton Templeton identifies this as a distinction between education and training, something I imagine he struggled with two hundred years ago while attending Ohio University. While it is sad that we continue to struggle with the same issues today, I find solace in the fact that many of us have in the past, and will in the future, successfully circumnavigate the mine field of education to become autonomous, free-thinking individuals. I think John Newton Templeton wouldn't have it any other way.

Free Man of Color was originally produced by Victory Gardens Theater, Chicago, Illinois, Dennis Zacek, artistic director. This world premiere production was in association with Ohio University Bicentennial Celebration, Athens, Ohio, 2004. The production was directed by Andrea J. Dymond and the cast was as follows:

Jane Wilson . . . . Shelley Delaney*
John Newton Templeton . . . . Anthony Fleming III*
Robert Wilson . . . . Gary Houston*

Denotes a member of Actor's Equity Association, the union of professional stage actors and managers.

PRODUCTION STAFF

Set Design . . . . Tim Morrison, USA
Costume Design . . . . Michelle Tesdall
Lighting Design . . . . Mary McDonald Badger, USA
Sound Design/Original Composition . . . . Joe Cerqua
Production Stage Manager . . . . Rita Vreeland, AEA

FREE MAN OF COLOR

A Play in Two Acts
For Two Men and One Woman

CHARACTERS

JOHN NEWTON TEMPLETON . . . . 20-year-old ex-slave

ROBERT WILSON . . middle-aged white university president

JANE WILSON . . . . Robert's somewhat younger wife

TIME: 1824 to 1828.

PLACE: Athens, Ohio.

ACT ONE

SCENE ONE

On stage are two chairs left and right. ROBERT WIL-SON sits in one of the chairs, JOHN NEWTON TEMPLETON sits in the other. A very rustic rendition of "Amazing Grace" plays in the background. When the music ends, WILSON stands.

WILSON *(to audience)*. Most distinguished assembled guests, trustees, gentlemen, at this point in the program, I present to you John Newton Templeton. The topic on which he will speak to you today is titled "The Claims of Liberia." Mister Templeton. *(WILSON exits.)*

JOHN *(to audience)*. "Non solum verba falsa sunt mala ipsa, sed etiam malo infligunt animam." For those of you who don't know, that was not "The Claims of Liberia." It was Latin. Plato. Roughly translated, it means, "False words are not only evil in themselves, but they inflict the soul with evil." That's what I was thinking on that day in 1828 when Reverend Wilson introduced me. I was thinking about my soul. Reverend Wilson was the president of Ohio University and judging by the look on his face, he and the seventy-five other assembled guests had fully expected to hear me speak on "The Claims of Liberia" because at one point in my life, I had been claimed by Liberia. 1828. Thirty-four years before the

9

end of slavery, I stood with my graduating class and wondered about my soul.

(WILSON enters. He has been traveling.)

WILSON. Here we are. I know it's a little different than what you're used to but we consider it to be a good home. Wife? *(He listens. There is no answer.)* I hope she's feeling better. She hasn't been in what you would call the best of health.

JOHN. Sorry to hear that.

WILSON. Have to be careful nowadays. We've had our share of the cholera. Yellow fever. Scarlet fever and smallpox. *(He calls through the window.)* Wife! *(No answer.)* I hope she didn't walk into town again. Woman has a stubborn streak in her. Won't let anybody do anything for her. I usually have a friend check on her while I'm gone. Make sure she's all right, drive her into town if she needs it, but she'd rather walk and it's too far to walk. Town is that way, north, about four miles. We'll go in tomorrow.

JOHN. Tomorrow?

WILSON *(calling)*. Wife?

JOHN. What about my papers?

WILSON. Your papers?

JOHN. I need to get my papers in order.

WILSON. We'll take care of that tomorrow, when we go into town.

JOHN. The law says—

WILSON. I know what the law says. Don't worry about the law. The law is my concern. The only thing I want you to be concerned about is your studies. You will begin your studies with nine other students and you will be treated the exact same as everyone else. Is that clear?

JOHN. Yes sir.

WILSON. You clear on what will be expected of you?

JOHN. Yes sir.

WILSON. Let's go over it again. How do you plan to start each day?

JOHN. With prayers at sunrise.

WILSON. Breakfast?

JOHN. Breakfast by six.

WILSON. Followed by...

JOHN. Morning recitations.

WILSON. Then comes?

JOHN. Morning lecture, then study until noon. Dinner will be from noon to one-thirty after which we begin afternoon recitations followed by afternoon lecture and study until supper. Supper is at five-thirty, followed by a half hour of relaxation and then evening debate.

WILSON. Good, John. Very good. Now, your first year will consist of the study of mathematics, science, and philosophy. Your second year will consist of the study of Latin, Hebrew, and Greek. In your third year, you will be expected to apply for admission into the Athenian Literary Society in addition to continuing your studies in Greek. And in your fourth year, you will prepare for your comprehensive exams.

JOHN. Yes sir.

WILSON. Tell me something, John. Why do you think it's important that you study Greek?

JOHN. Why?

WILSON. That's right. Why? Why Greek?

JOHN. Greek is an important language, sir.

WILSON. Is that your answer? Greek is an important language? That's not an answer, John. That's circular logic based upon the original premise. "Why is the horse white? Because it's a white horse." Does that make sense? No. All you did was chew my question and then feed it back to me in the form of an answer, but that's not an answer. You haven't added anything to it. Nothing but your own saliva and I do not care for the taste of your saliva, John. Now let's try it again. Why is it important that you study Greek?

JOHN. I don't know.

WILSON. Didn't you study Greek at Ripley?

JOHN. Yes sir.

WILSON. Didn't they tell you why you were studying Greek?

JOHN. They said it was important.

WILSON. Of course it's important, John. I want you to tell me why it's important.

JOHN. It's important for us to understand our language?

WILSON. Not unless you consider language to be the end and language is not the end, it's merely a means to the end. Think about the white horse. Can you ride the words "white horse"? Will those words carry you to the store? Do you have to feed those words? No, those words are merely a representation of the thing itself. Those words do not have a heartbeat, those words will not leave filth in the middle of the road. Our goal is not to understand the words, John. Our goal is to understand all of the things the words represent. Have you ever studied the Bible?

JOHN. Of course I have.

WILSON. In what language did you study the Bible?

JOHN. English.

WILSON. Are you suggesting to me that Matthew, Mark, Timothy and Samuel wrote their testaments in English?

JOHN. No sir.

WILSON. In what language did they write?

JOHN. They wrote in Hebrew, sir. And Greek.

WILSON. That's right. And unless you are studying the Bible in Hebrew and Greek, you're not studying the Bible. You're studying what somebody else has said the Bible says, and while King James may have been a very honest man, I'd rather not stake my soul and the souls of all men on his judgment. That's the reason the study of Greek is so important, John, that's why the study of Hebrew and Latin is important, so that we may study the actual word of God in its original form. Remember, only by studying the origins of a thing, can one discern that thing's true meaning.

JOHN. Only by studying the origin of a thing—

(JANE enters. She stops and surveys the situation.)

JANE. What's this?

WILSON. This is John Templeton. I'm sorry, John *Newton* Templeton. John, this is Missus Wilson.

JOHN. Pleased to meet you, ma'am.

JANE. You promised we were not going to do this.

WILSON. Do what, dear?

JANE. Take in runaways.

WILSON. He's not a runaway. He's a free man.

JANE. Legal free or liberated free?

WILSON. Legal free and he's here to go to school.

JANE. School?

WILSON. John, why don't you go out and get the rest of our things.

JOHN. Yes sir. *(JOHN exits.)*

JANE. Robert, what're you doing?

WILSON. Reverend Hopkins come by while I was gone?

JANE. 'Course he came by, every day he came by. Can't get rid of the man.

WILSON. I asked him to check on you while I was gone.

JANE. And I told you that I don't need anybody to check on me. Now I would like to know what that boy is doing here.

WILSON. He was at Ripley with Reverend Williamson. The boy is smart, Jane. He knows philosophy, mathematics, basic Greek and Latin. And the boy is strong. He had never ridden a horse before in his life, not until he got on one to come here. But after the first day, he was riding like a professional.

JANE. You taught him how to ride?

WILSON. First thirty miles to Hillsboro were kind of hard on him. But after I showed him a few things he got the hang of it. By the time we could see the first of the seven hills of Athens, he was riding like he had been born in the saddle.

JANE. What is he doing here, Robert?

WILSON. I told you. He's here to go to school.

JANE. You going up against the law for him?

WILSON. Nothing in the law that says that he can't be here.

JANE. And that's the reason you're doing it? Because nothing says you can't?

WILSON. We minister to everyone else in this world.

JANE. We minister to colored.

WILSON. Never with substance. We preach to them, sure, we offer them the word of God, but never has anyone offered them the means by which they can obtain that word on their own.

JANE. Where's he supposed to live while he's here?

WILSON. I thought he could stay here with us for a while.

JANE. Where here?

WILSON. Spare room.

JANE. We don't have a spare room.

WILSON. The room isn't being used, Jane. He can sleep there. Won't be for long. Only a month or so.

JANE. A month?

WILSON. After folks get used to the idea of him being around, we can move him into the edifice with the other students if you like.

JANE. With the gentleman from Virginia? The two gentlemen from Kentucky? You think that these men are going to sleep in the same room as a black?

WILSON. Won't be the same room.

JANE. Under the same roof. You expect these men to share a roof with a black who is not washing their clothes and serving them dinner? Is that what you're asking me to believe?

WILSON. If it doesn't work out, we can find him a room in town someplace, I don't know. The where of the matter is not important at this point.

JANE. The where of the matter is the most important. Everything in this world revolves around the where.

WILSON. If you don't want him here and if he has a problem in the edifice, we'll find a room for him in town.

(JOHN enters with saddlebags.)

JANE. Is he registered?

WILSON. We'll take care of that tomorrow.

JANE. Does he have money to register?

WILSON. The university is sovereign. As long as he's in our charge, he's not subject to local ordinances.

JANE. Nobody in town is going to put him up unless he's registered.

WILSON. Why must you see darkness wherever you look?

JANE. Because my life has been shrouded in darkness. I've lived in darkness for so long, it's become a friend of mine, the only companion I have.

JOHN. Pardon me, sir, but if you would tell me where to unhitch and water the horses, I'll take care of it.

WILSON. I'll take care of it, John. You get yourself cleaned up, get yourself something to eat.

JANE. Folks in town are not going to want him here unless he's registered, Robert.

WILSON. Folks in town don't have a say in the matter.

JANE. You can't continue to ignore who these people are and what they believe in.

WILSON. I don't care what they believe in. John will be here whether they like it or not. My charge doesn't come from the folks in town. I receive my charge from the trustees and the state legislature. I answer to them and after them, I answer only to God. I do not have to answer to a bunch of provincial merchants, landowners and pig farmers.

JANE. You may not have to answer to them. But we do have to live with them.

WILSON. I think we've been very charitable neighbors.

JANE. When it benefits you. You won't consider anything that doesn't benefit you or the university.

WILSON. I've considered many proposals.

JANE. What about the tent?

WILSON. I have no objections to that tent.

JANE. Within the square?

WILSON. Anyplace outside the gates.

JANE. Outside the gates.

WILSON. It's for the amusement and entertainment of the locals. If they want to be amused and entertained by abominations, they can erect as many circus tents as they please. Anyplace outside of the square.

JANE. There's nothing evil about the circus, Robert. They come in, they set up their tents, they tell stories. You go there and listen to stories about people and places far away from here. That's all it is. It's a diversion. It might be nice to have a bit of diversion around here.

WILSON. My students do not need diversion. My students need earnest uninterrupted study.

JANE. There are people here other than your students.

WILSON. What people. Who?

JANE. People.

WILSON. I want you to tell me whose need for entertainment and diversion you think is more important than the education of my students.

JANE. Nobody's. I'm sorry I brought it up.

WILSON. Draw some water for the boy so he can get cleaned up. And he needs something different to wear. Look around and see if we've got some clothes that'll fit him. Shirt, pants, maybe a hat.

JANE. There's nothing here that will fit him.

WILSON. Why don't you look see?

JANE. I don't have to look see. I know. There is nothing here that will fit him.

WILSON. Draw him some water so he can get cleaned up. I'll be back in a bit. *(WILSON exits.)*

JOHN. If it's all the same to you, ma'am, I can draw my own water.

JANE. Of course you can. You can and you will. I will not draw water for you while you're in this house.

JOHN. No, ma'am.

JANE. Washbasin is in there under the table.

JOHN. Yes, ma'am. *(He moves to exit. He stops.)* I didn't come here to cause trouble, ma'am. Reverend Wilson asked me if I wanted to come here and go to school. He said he was looking for young men of high moral content; young men who would eventually serve in honor of the public good. I believe I am such a man. Reverend Wilson also believes that I am such a man, and I am grateful that he's given me the chance to prove it.

JANE. So...you want to serve the public good.

JOHN. Yes, ma'am.

JANE. And just how do you plan to do that...what's your name again?

JOHN. John, ma'am.

JANE. John what?

JOHN. John Newton Templeton.

JANE. Just how do you plan to serve the public good, Mister John Newton Templeton?

JOHN. I'm not quite sure, ma'am. I thought that maybe I'd become a preacher like the Reverend. Spread the word of God. Maybe one day, even open my own school. School for colored. That's what I'd like to do.

JANE. That's very sweet of you. Tell me something, Mister John Newton Templeton, you born free? Or is liberation a relatively new experience for you?

JOHN. I was freed when I was seven, eight years old, ma'am.

JANE. You don't remember the day?

JOHN. I remember the day. It was June 17th, 1813. That was the day the good Reverend Master Thomas Williamson of Spartanburg, South Carolina, died. Yes, ma'am, I remember the day. What I meant to say was, I don't know how old I was on that day. I was born the winter of '06-'07. Don't know which month, all I know is that I was born during a hard snowfall, which is rare for South Carolina. That would've made me seven, maybe eight years old on the day that me, my momma, and my daddy were freed. Yes, ma'am, I remember the day. Just don't know how old I was on that day.

JANE. What're you doing here?

JOHN. I believe I just told you, ma'am. I come here to prove myself.

JANE. You didn't come here, Mister John Newton Templeton. You were brought here. What I'm trying to figure out is if you know the reason you were brought here, 'cause it sounds like you don't know.

JOHN. All right then. I was brought here to prove myself. Reverend says that I'm special, because of my birth. Reverend says that if I came here, I'd be treated the same as everybody else. I'd like to believe that I'm at least as good as most men. Better than some. Not as good as others.

JANE. You probably think you're pretty smart, don't you?

JOHN. Smart?

JANE. Intelligent.

JOHN. I would like to think I possess a modicum of intelligence, yes.

JANE. You don't sound so smart to me. Not so smart at all. See, your desire to prove yourself only put you in a place where you could be seen. But that is not the reason you were brought here, and make no mistake, you were not only brought here but brought here for a reason. You were chosen, Mister Templeton. Out of all the rest of them out there, they chose you. You might as well had been standing on the block. "How about dis one chere?" "Issy healthy?" "Healthy as a mule, looka him kicking." "How 'bout his mind? Issy crazy?" "Nope, dis here nigger has a nice, even temperament. Look at dose eyes. Who can resist dose puppy-dog eyes?" Yes sir, Mister Templeton, they fished you out of a lake of misery. And I bet you thought you were pretty lucky, when they pulled you outta that putrid lake. But what you should've done before patting yourself on the back for being so lucky, what you should've done was ask the reason why. If you knew the reason why, that lake of misery you were swimming in might not have looked so bad.

JOHN. I know the reason why.

JANE. Do you? You come here to be a houseboy? That the reason you're here?

JOHN. I come here to prove to this world that the colored race is capable of climbing to the same heights— *(He stops himself.)*

JANE. Same heights as white?

JOHN. Yes, ma'am. Same heights as white.

JANE. Is that what you believe? Or is that what somebody told you?

JOHN. That's what I believe.

JANE. And you think that's the reason Reverend brought you here? To prove that colored is as good as white?

JOHN. I know that's the reason he brought me here.

JANE. Is that what he said to you?

JOHN. Is that what he said to me?

JANE. Did he come out and say those words? That he brought you here to prove that colored was as good as white?

JOHN. Maybe not those exact words.

JANE. Then you didn't hear him say it.

JOHN. Didn't have to hear him say it exactly. I know what's in his heart, what's in his mind.

JANE. So, you supernatural on top of everything else? You able to look inside a man's heart and his mind? That's quite a trick. With skills like that, what you need to go to school for?

JOHN. Don't have to be supernatural to divine what's in a man's heart. All you have to do is listen to him speak. I know what he believes.

JANE. You know what? You remind me a little bit of my youngest boy, David. He was ignorant, you're ignorant. Just a fool. No idea of what's going on around them. Huge wheels turning, grinding the world into shattered bits of bone and shredded flesh. And you, like him, are ignorant, oblivious to the sounds, the screams. Tell me something, Mister John Newton Templeton. What would happen if you found out that the reason you were brought here was different than the reason you think? What would that do to your intelligent colored thinking?

JOHN. I don't understand your meaning.

JANE. You think you as good as white?

JOHN. I've studied Latin, Greek, and many of the classics in the canon.

JANE. I asked if you thought you were as good as white.

JOHN. That depends.

JANE. Depends on what?

JOHN. Depends on what you mean by "good."

JANE. Are you trying to play a word game with me? Is that what you're trying to do?

JOHN. I'm trying to understand your meaning, ma'am.

JANE. I asked if you thought you were as good as white. It's not a very complex question.

JOHN. I believe that, given the chance, I can achieve anything that a white man can achieve. And that's the reason I'm here. To prove that I'm a man of high moral content. A man who is capable of serving in honor of the public good.

JANE. Oh, you will serve. Make no mistake about that. I'm sure you will serve nicely. *(JANE exits.)*

JOHN *(to audience).* I hated that woman. Every time I looked at her, I kept visualizing my fingers wrapped around her throat and you don't have to tell me: I know, that was not a very good visualization. So I made up my mind to stay as far away from her as possible. I started to think of the many ways I was going to avoid her. Unfortunately, I wasn't able to think quite fast enough.

(WILSON enters.)

WILSON. One thing you have to understand about the others, particularly the gentlemen from South Carolina as well as the gentlemen from Virginia and Kentucky: they've never been around anybody like you before. I mean, they've been around plenty of blacks, but they were always blacks that they or somebody else owned. You can understand, it must be very difficult for them.

JOHN. I can imagine.

WILSON. And sleep is a very important part of a man's life, John. Even God had to rest. If these men are unable to sleep in the same room...

JOHN. Under the same roof. Not the same room. We'd be sleeping under the same roof.

WILSON. Under the same roof, you're right. These are their shortcomings, John. You have to understand.

JOHN. What about me? They need to rest, what about me? I need rest too.

WILSON. Haven't you been resting comfortably here in the house?

JOHN. 'Course I have.

WILSON. Then what's the urgency? You've been comfortable here in the house, we've been comfortable having you here. There's no problem. There's no urgency.

JOHN. I should be in the edifice with the other men.

WILSON. Of course you should be. Unfortunately, the world is full of should be's, John. And it wouldn't be so bad to live here in the house with Jane and me. In fact, Jane would like it, to have somebody else around. She needs somebody to keep her company. Somebody to drive her into town when she needs it.

JOHN. No sir, it wouldn't be right.

WILSON. What wouldn't be right?

JOHN. You said if I came here, I'd come here as a charity student and that charity students didn't have to pay.

WILSON. That wouldn't change. You still wouldn't have to pay.

JOHN. If I was in the edifice, I'd be with other men, some of whom also didn't have to pay. But living here in the house with you and Missus Wilson, I wouldn't feel right, not paying. I'd at least want to pay for my room, pay for my meals.

WILSON. All right. You stay here with me and Missus Wilson, and in exchange, you can do a little work around the house. What do you think about that? Cut wood, clean squirrels, rabbits, serve dinner, that sort of thing.

JOHN. Like a houseboy?

WILSON. That's an unfortunate way to put it.

JOHN. Unfortunate but true. I'd be a houseboy.

WILSON. I'd prefer not to use that terminology, John. I'd prefer to look at it a bit differently. We'll call it something else. Something a bit kinder.

JOHN. Something like what?

WILSON. Student servant. That's what you'll be. You'd be a student servant.

JOHN. Just because we call it something different doesn't change the fact of what it is.

WILSON. We're not trying to change the fact of what it is. We're calling it something different because it will be something different. If you were a houseboy you would do exactly as I told you to do when I told you to do it. If you were a houseboy, you would follow my orders, without question or hesitation or face severe consequences. But that's not who you will be, John. You will be a student servant, almost like one of the family. Student servant means that you're a student, first and foremost. Your primary duty will be to attend classes and to keep up with your studies. Student servant means that you and I together will decide what your secondary duties will be. If you don't find cutting wood and serving dinner to be acceptable, we'll find something else for you to do. Something that you do find acceptable. Like taking care of the horses. You said you liked being around horses. What do you think about that? You can take care of the horses and we could continue your riding lessons. You and I, we could go out once a week riding. What do you think?

JOHN. That would be nice. Yes.

WILSON. Then it's settled. You'll stay here in the house with us and in exchange, take care of the horses. Now tell me something. Elections coming up. If you were allowed to vote, who would you vote for?

JOHN. Sir?

WILSON. I'm sure you've kept up with politics and must have formed an opinion on this debacle of an election.

JOHN. No sir.

WILSON. No you haven't formed an opinion or no you don't keep up with politics?

JOHN. No, I haven't formed an opinion.

WILSON. We're talking about the future of the United States of America here and you haven't formed an opinion?

JOHN. I learned a long time ago not to waste my time thinking about what I would do in a situation that I know will never happen. Why should I waste my time thinking about who I would vote for in a world in which I cannot vote?

WILSON. But that's where you're wrong. You can vote, John. However, at this point in time, you're not allowed to vote. There's a difference.

JOHN. None that I can see.

WILSON. Can't vote means that you're physically or mentally unable to vote. Not allowed to vote means that you're physically capable of voting, but just not permitted. Understand?

JOHN. Physically capable...

WILSON. But not permitted.

JOHN. What would happen if I went into town and tried to vote? Would somebody block my way?

WILSON. Probably.

JOHN. Would I be beaten?

WILSON. Most likely.

JOHN. Killed?

WILSON. You're drifting from the point, John.

JOHN. I thought the point was whether or not I was physically capable of voting. If somebody blocked my way, beat me and tried to kill me, I would say that I would not be, at that point in time, physically capable, so not only am I not allowed, but I can't.

WILSON. All right. Let's put it this way. If you were allowed and if you could, who would you vote for?

JOHN. I don't know, sir. I think they're both very fine gentlemen.

WILSON. But they're nothing alike. Adams is the son of a Federalist. He was born with a silver spoon in his mouth. His daddy was president and some think that makes him qualified to be president too. Jackson is a military hero. No silver spoon here, no sir, he was born with a shovel in his hand. Jackson is a self-made man who never asked anybody for anything. If you could choose between the two, which one would you choose?

JOHN. All things being equal, I imagine that if I could vote, I would vote for that Mister Adams fella.

WILSON. Adams? Why Adams?

JOHN. He's against slave owning. His daddy was against slave owning.

WILSON. So you do know something about the candidates.

JOHN. All I know is that Mister Adams is against slave owning so if I had to choose, I would choose him.

WILSON. That all you know about the man? That he's against slave owning?

JOHN. Isn't that enough?

WILSON. To make a decision like that based upon a single issue is selfish and irresponsible, John. The future of a nation cannot rest upon a single issue.

JOHN. What other issues are there?

WILSON. I thought you said you kept up with politics.

JOHN. I never said that. You said that.

WILSON. There are plenty of issues, John. There's the issue of the Monroe Doctrine; is it good policy or merely a prelude to war? There's the question of the Twelfth Amendment; should the House of Representatives be deciding who our next president should be? And Andrew Jackson is one of the founding members of the ACS, did you know that?

JOHN. The ACS?

WILSON. American Colonization Society, John. They want to do great things for you and your people.

JOHN. They want to ship us all back to Africa.

WILSON. That was a very uninformed and uneducated opinion. What the ACS wants to do is establish a civilized, democratic, Christian society where your people can live sovereign. A place where your people can rule themselves, John. A place where your people can determine their own destiny. A place that looks a lot like America.

JOHN. Why should the colored of America have to leave America in order to live in a place that looks like America?

WILSON. Why should the colored of America be any different than all the other people of this world? Men have had to roam the face of this earth in search of a place to call home for thousands of years. My father did it. When the English came to Ireland, they took my father's land, they burned his house, they tried to relocate him and my mother to some remote strip of barren land that couldn't even yield a single potato or carrot. He tried to fight and when it became clear that he couldn't win, he and my mother stole upon a ship bound for America. I was born one year later in Lincoln County, North Carolina. And my father was not the only man who has had to do this. World history is replete with people searching for the land of promise, a place to call home. Think of Moses. Exodus, chapter 3, verse 10, and God said to Moses, "Come, I will send you to the Pharaoh that you may bring forth my people, the sons of Israel, out of Egypt." To say that all the ACS wants to do is send your people back to Africa reveals your ignorance, John. What the ACS wants to do is to free your people from bondage.

JOHN. Perhaps I should study the issue a bit more.

WILSON. Perhaps you should. Your master freed you at a very young age, but only through training and education will you be able to retain your freedom.

(JANE enters.)

JANE. Tent's going up on the green. Half the town's turned out to see it. They say they have women who do trick riding, bareback and saddled. That's what I wanna see. Women on horseback. I'll tell you, there hasn't been this much excitement around here since Missus Mavis' cow gave birth to that two-headed calf.

WILSON. Abominations.

JANE. Pardon me?

WILSON. All of it's an abomination.

JANE. Have to admit, the two-headed calf was a bit strange. I want to thank you again for allowing them to put up the tents.

WILSON. I asked you not to thank me.

JANE. Now, Robert, there's no need to be shy. You did a good deed, and I believe in giving credit where credit is due.

WILSON. It wasn't a good deed.

JANE. I know you were against the idea...

WILSON. Still am. Nothing's changed.

JANE. Whenever a man goes against what he believes in order to make somebody else happy, it should be recognized.

WILSON. I didn't do it to make anybody happy.

JANE. You made me happy.

WILSON. That's not the reason I did it.

JANE. Whatever reason you did it, I want to thank you.

WILSON. It was Miller. He wouldn't give John his papers. He said he had to pay a five-hundred-dollar bond and nobody has five hundred dollars. I told him, I said the university is a sovereign entity. As long as this boy is in the charge of the university, we didn't need to pay a bond, but he wasn't having it. Said the way he read the law, the boy has to pay his bond, whether he's in the charge of the university or not. Finally, I asked him, what would happen if the university allowed the circus to put up its tents on the green. And you know what he said? He said that if we allowed the circus to put up its tents on the green that he might be inclined to read the law the same way I read the law, so I agreed to it. But just 'cause I agreed to it doesn't change how I feel about it. I'm still against it and would appreciate it if you would stop thanking me for it at every turn. Every time I hear you say it, it puts a bad taste in my mouth.

JANE. And here I thought you had committed an act of compassion. Turns out, you had to be forced into it.

WILSON. You consider this to be an act of compassion? Having a hand in helping folks gawk at a collection of misery, misfortunes, and abominations is an act of compassion? Or is it entertainment? Isn't that what you called it? Misery, misfortune and abominations here for your amusement and entertainment.

JANE. I learned early in life to love life's bounty, be it misery, misfortune, or abominations.

WILSON. You love abominations? Is that what you're saying?

JANE. I don't think you really want me to answer that, do you? I washed the boy's bedclothes. They're out hanging on the line. When is he going to be moving into the edifice with the other students?

JOHN *(to audience)*. Sure enough, the next day, a wagon rolled through town with a washboard jug band on the back. The band played music announcing to anyone who didn't already know that that the circus had officially come to town. The same day that wagon rolled into town, Reverend Wilson rolled out of town. Said he had to meet with some men in Chillicothe but I thought the real reason was that he didn't want to be here when the circus arrived. The circus consisted of an assortment of wonderful oddities and delights. There was a man who had six fingers on each hand, a woman who was covered with hair from head to toe, and a boy who could twist himself into all kinds of unnatural-looking shapes. And of course, they had the women who did trick horseback riding, bareback and saddled. They also had an elephant, a lion, a zebra that they called a striped horse, and an ostrich that caused a lot of excitement. I don't think anybody had ever seen a seven-foot bird before. I think a whole lot of folks wanted to eat it. But by far, the most popular attraction, the one thing that amazed young and old alike, was Mongo, the Trained Ape. Mongo was an ape who had been trained to perform various tricks. He drank water from a cup. He smoked a cigar. He sat at a table, and when it came time to eat, he used a spoon. This was a particularly remarkable feat, especially when you consider that at least half of the population of town at the time did not use or even own a spoon. But the most disconcerting part of this animal's act was that they had outfitted him with a hat, shirt with a collar, and pair of trousers. Mongo attracted fairly moderate attention for almost a week. But this was nothing like the sensation caused later when, late one night, somebody sneaked into the encampment and defaced the board that stood in front of Mongo's tent. To the shock of some, and to the delight of others, on the board announcing Mongo the

Trained Ape, somebody had crossed out the name Mongo and had written, in its place, John Newton Templeton.

(JANE enters.)

JANE. What you reading?

JOHN. Cicero.

JANE. Can I see?

JOHN. It's in Latin.

JANE. I didn't ask you what language it was in. *(JOHN hands JANE the book. She starts to page through it.)* I need you to go into town and pick up a few things.

JOHN. I can drive you if you want to go.

JANE. Did I tell you I needed a ride? Go see Mister Burke. He's going to give you some hog's blood.

JOHN. Hog's blood?

JANE. For the garden. Keep the animals away. That's gonna be one of your jobs now. Keeping the animals out of the garden.

JOHN. What kind of animals?

JANE. Deer mostly.

JOHN. Reverend said my job was to take care of the horses.

JANE. And take care of the garden. That's now another one of your jobs. They have deer where you come from in South Carolina?

JOHN. I know about deer.

JANE. Then you know that they have to be kept away or they'll get in and eat up the fruit of four months of our labor. And what they don't eat, they'll trample into the ground. From now on, your job will be keeping them from doing that.

JOHN. With hog's blood?

JANE. You spread it around. Make a big circle around the garden, around the house. Makes the whole place smell of death. Animals don't like the smell of death.

JOHN. Some animals. Others might be attracted to it.

JANE. I don't know of any animals that are attracted to the smell of blood.

JOHN. Bobcat. Bear. Coyote.

JANE. You don't know much about the wilderness, do you?

JOHN. I know that the smell of blood will attract vermin.

JANE. Vermin maybe, but not bobcat, bear and coyote. Bobcat, bear and coyote are killers. They're not interested in what's already dead. They're looking to kill something. They kill, they eat. That means that they're looking for something alive. The more alive, the better. Now go do like I told you. The man's name is Mister Burke.

JOHN. May I have my book back, please?

JANE. You'll get it after you do like I told you.

JOHN. If I took it with me, I could read along the way.

JANE. You can read and ride at the same time?

JOHN. I'm getting fairly good at it.

JANE. Multitalented. You see the newspaper? Your man was appointed president.

JOHN. My man?

JANE. Adams. Reverend's going to be disappointed when he hears about that.

JOHN. How did Adams get to be my man?

JANE. Weren't you pulling for him?

JOHN. I wasn't pulling for anybody.

JANE. You told Reverend you wanted him to win.

JOHN. I said that if I had to choose, I would choose him.

JANE. 'Cause he's against slavery?

JOHN. Isn't that good enough reason?

JANE. All I did was ask a question. You'd choose Adams 'cause he's against slavery?

JOHN. That's right.

JANE. The Reverend and Andrew Jackson went to school together. That means that the three of you are practically kinsmen.

JOHN. Kinsmen?

JANE. They're from North Carolina, you're from South Carolina.

JOHN. Andrew Jackson killed over six hundred Indian men, women and children. He is not my kinsman.

JANE. But isn't that how men forge their bond-ships? Using pieces of land and boundaries drawn on a map.

JOHN. Some men.

JANE. All men. Everything in this world is about the where of the matter. Look at the men from Kentucky. They are united in the fact that they hate the men from Virginia. The Virginians got their own handshake, their own song. And you, the Reverend, and Andrew Jackson are all from the Carolinas. Seems to me that if you could choose, you would have chosen him, he being your kinsman and all.

JOHN. But I can't choose now and couldn't have chosen then. So who I would have chosen, if I could have chosen, is irrelevant, now isn't it?

JANE. That's why I am so perplexed. Seeing how your opinion on the matter is absolutely irrelevant, I don't understand why you didn't just shuffle yo' feet, nod yo' head and agree with the Reverend.

JOHN. This may come as a shock to you, but I am a free thinker. I don't shuffle my feet or nod my head in sycophantic agreement with any man.

JANE. Sycophantic?

JOHN. That's right. Sycophantic. You know what it means?

JANE. I know what it means. Do you?

JOHN. It means I am not some bent-back slave who stands at the elbow of the master agreeing with everything he says. I am a free man. A free man of color. Now if you would please give me my book back...

JANE. Then how come you didn't pay your bond?

JOHN. My what?

JANE. The law says that every free man of color has to post a bond upon entering the state.

JOHN. I know what the law says.

JANE. Then how come you didn't pay?

JOHN. Reverend says that the university is sovereign. Reverend says as long as I'm here, I'm sovereign.

JANE. Reverend says Reverend says. What do you say?

JOHN. I agree with the Reverend. The university is sovereign. That means as long as I'm here, I'm sovereign.

JANE. If you consider yourself sovereign living here and now, then you must have also considered yourself sovereign when you were a slave living on that plantation back in South Carolina.

JOHN. I think there's a difference.

JANE. Do you? Do you remember your life before liberation?

JOHN. What kind of question is that?

JANE. It must've been hard work for a boy of seven, eight years old, picking all that cotton.

JOHN. I didn't pick cotton.

JANE. Then you were a pickaninny.

JOHN. A pickaninny.

JANE. A slave living on a cotton plantation who didn't pick cotton is called a pickaninny.

JOHN. I know what it's called.

JANE. 'Cause you didn't pick any. I'm guessing you ran around half-naked, maybe wearing a burlap bag if you were lucky.

JOHN. I didn't wear no burlap bag.

JANE. You had nice clothes.

JOHN. Hand-me-downs.

JANE. Hand-me-downs?

JOHN. From the son of Reverend Master Williamson.

JANE. Nice clothes. Better than what you're wearing now, I'm guessing.

JOHN. Somewhat better.

JANE. What about the beatings? You must've been beaten on a regular basis.

JOHN. May I have my book back, please?

JANE. Answer my question first. Were you beat as a little boy?

JOHN. I was never beaten.

JANE. Were you hungry?

JOHN. We were well taken care of.

JANE. They teach you to read?

JOHN. Like I said. We were well taken care of.

JANE. You didn't pick cotton, you didn't work in the fields, you had nice clothes, at least better than what you're wearing now. Plenty to eat, never mistreated, they even schooled you, boy, taught you how to read. So explain to me the difference between your life then and your life now.

JOHN. That's easy. You see, I have something now that I didn't have back then. Now I'm the one who makes the choices about my life. I control my direction and I control my destiny. I remember the first time I saw my daddy do that. My daddy was a carpenter. Supposed to have been one of the best around. Man came to my master's house one day and wanted to hire my daddy out. He said they were building a new city called Washington and they were looking for the best masons, the best carpenters they could find. By then, my master, Master Williamson, had found religion. He had received what he called second sight. He was no longer Master Williamson. He had become Reverend Master Williamson and no longer hired his slaves out to anybody who had a dollar. So Reverend Master Williamson did something he had never done before. He told the man that he would have to ask my daddy and then let my daddy decide if he wanted to go help build this new city or not. My daddy listened to the man talk about the great buildings they were building. A tower, a rotunda, a great house. And then, at the end of it all, my daddy carefully considered, nodded his head and said if it was that great, that he wanted to go there and be a part of it all. I had never seen my daddy do that before. To consider, nod his head, then decide. I thought it was the most wonderful thing in the world. Now, I have that power and that's the difference between then and now. Now, I have the power to consider, nod my head, then decide.

JANE. I can't tell if you're mixing up this stew for my benefit or if you actually believe this hog slop you're trying to serve me on a silver platter. You do not have the power to decide anything that happens in your life. You gave up that right when you failed to pay your bond. When you failed to pay your bond, you became a charge of the university. We are responsible for you and everything you do. That means you can nod your head all you want but you're not making any decisions, not around here. That's the reason folks in town wanted you to pay your bond. Ohio is a free state. They don't like the idea of slavery. Neither do they like the idea of indentured servitude.

JOHN. I'm not an indentured servant.

JANE. You work here, you don't get paid, the university is responsible for you. You're indentured, whether you like it or not. That means that the only difference between now and back then is back then, you were a little better dressed because back then you got hand-me-downs from your master's son, but that's the only difference. Now go into town and do like I told you. You'll get your book when you get back.

SCENE TWO

JOHN and WILSON.

WILSON. I saw what somebody wrote on that board in front of that monkey cage. When did it happen?

JOHN. Couple weeks ago.

WILSON. It's been like that since I left? Nobody took it down?

JOHN. Not if it's still there.

WILSON. I'm sorry, John. I allowed them to bring their wickedness here. I knew something like this would happen.

JOHN. It's not your fault.

WILSON. I'm gonna go see Miller and I'm gonna give them twenty-four hours to tear down that tent, pack their wagons and get off of government property. If they're not gone by the morning, I will go out and tear down that tent myself.

JOHN. With all respect, sir, you tear down that tent, all you gonna do is antagonize folks.

WILSON. Folks need to be antagonized. They can't do something like this without expecting retribution. To compare a man to an ape. A man is not an ape.

JOHN. But we don't even know if they're the ones who did it.

WILSON. Who else could have done it?

JOHN. Most folks in town can't even read, much less write, and you saw the sign. That sign was done up in a very nice hand. Most of the folks I met had to have somebody read to them what it said and a lot of them didn't find it funny. The only folks who found it funny were the folks here on campus.

WILSON. What folks?

JOHN. The gentleman from Virginia, Mister Drake. And the gentleman from Kentucky, Mister Ward. They thought it was funny. In fact, Mister Ward was the one who told me about it.

WILSON. You suggesting that Mister Ward did this?

JOHN. I'm suggesting that perhaps we've been too harsh in our judgment of the folks in town. I don't think they had a hand in this.

WILSON. They knew the sign was there. And nobody, not one man stepped forward to remove it. The tent goes the first thing in the morning.

JOHN. What about my papers?

WILSON. What about them?

JOHN. Miller agreed to waive my bond in exchange for the right to put up that tent. If you make them take it down...

WILSON. It'll send a message that we are serious about you being here. It'll send a message that we will not tolerate any type of tomfoolery.

JOHN. What happens if they revoke my papers?

WILSON. That's not gonna happen.

JOHN. What if it does?

WILSON. Half the town owes the university money for lands they've leased. If they threaten to revoke your papers, I will be forced to demand full payment for every lease that's now in arrears. And they can't pay, John. They don't have the money to pay. I don't think you have to worry.

JOHN. I don't like this. I don't like being in the middle of this.

WILSON. You're in the middle, John, whether you like it or not. You know who I met with when I was in Chillicothe? I met with members of the ACS. Congress just gave the ACS $100,000, John. They're ready to charter a ship. They're ready to purchase iron works for a sawmill and a gristmill, tools, muskets, gunpowder, fishing equipment, everything men would need to settle a new land. The only thing they need now is someone to govern that land, and I believe that someone is you.

JOHN. Me?

WILSON. There are three other men in this country, free men of color, who are receiving education and training to undertake this endeavor. There's one at Amherst, one at Bowdoin College, and one at Dartmouth. But you, John, you have something these other men don't. You have a mandate from God. I believe that you are the man God chose to lead his people to a new land.

JOHN. Liberia?

WILSON. Liberia.

JOHN. But I don't know anything about Liberia.

WILSON. The only thing you need to know is the word of God. Look at this area. The men who settled this area didn't know anything about the area before they came here. Twenty-five years ago, this was nothing but wilderness. No human habitation at all. Wild animals, deer, bobcats, and Indians. The men who came here knew nothing but the word of God. But we have blessed this land with civilization, culture, and education. We came here and brought God to a godless region. And that's what God is asking you to do, John. To lead your people through the wilderness to a new land. To bring God to a godless land.

JOHN. God is asking me to do this?

WILSON. All you have to do is look at your origins.

JOHN. What origins?

WILSON. The circumstances surrounding your birth, John.

JOHN. The snowfall?

WILSON. After the snowfall. What happened that summer, the summer after you were born?

JOHN. What do you mean?

WILSON. There was a man named Gabriel Prosser. You remember Gabriel Prosser?

JOHN. I remember.

WILSON. Who was he?

JOHN. A blacksmith. A slave.

WILSON. And what did Gabriel Prosser do?

JOHN. They said he tried to organize a revolt.

WILSON. Was the revolt successful?

JOHN. No.

WILSON. What happened?

JOHN. They were discovered.

WILSON. Discovered?

JOHN. He and thirty-five others.

WILSON. What happened after they were discovered, John?

JOHN. They were hanged. Thirty-six of them were hanged in the public square.

WILSON. Then what happened? *(JOHN doesn't answer.)* John? What happened after they hanged the men responsible for planning the revolt?

JOHN. After they hanged the men responsible for planning the revolt, the night riders came. They went from house to house. They took only the boys. The baby boys. All of the black-skinned, the brown-skinned, and the yellow-skinned baby boys.

WILSON. And what did they do with the baby boys?

JOHN. They killed them. They shot them. They drowned them in buckets. They cut their throats. They smashed in their skulls with stones. They ran them through with wooden stakes and stuck them to trees. They left shredded bits of bone and flesh scattered along the roadside that led to and from town.

WILSON. What happened to you?

JOHN. My mother said she tried to hide me but she couldn't hide me. She tried but my mistress, my mistress found me. She took me in. She hid me until the danger had passed.

WILSON. Your mistress may have been the one who hid you, but she was guided by the hand of God. It was God who saved you out of all the others who died.

JOHN. You think God saved me to go to Liberia?

WILSON. To lead your people to Liberia, John. It couldn't be any clearer if God himself appeared and wrote it on the wall.

JOHN. I always thought that I would be a preacher. Or a teacher. I had always imagined myself standing in front of a classroom full of colored children, little brown and black boys and girls. I always thought that was my purpose, that that was the reason God had saved me. I would have never imagined this.

WILSON. That's the reason I'm here. To teach you. To guide you. To open the door to the path of your true calling.

JOHN. Liberia?

WILSON. Liberia.

JOHN. What do I have to do?

WILSON. Keep up with your studies. The officers of the ACS will come here sometime next year. They want to meet you, talk to you, get to know you to decide if indeed you are the man they are looking for.

JOHN. They're not convinced?

WILSON. They don't know. Not like I know. But don't you worry. We'll convince them. In the meantime, I'm going to go get rid of that tent. I think you would agree that we cannot allow the future governor of Liberia to be compared to an ape.

JOHN. Reverend?

WILSON. Yes?

JOHN. One more thing. A small thing.

WILSON. What is it?

JOHN. I'm almost embarrassed to ask because I don't want to sound like I'm ungrateful...

WILSON. Spit it out, boy. What is it?

JOHN. I would like to be paid.

WILSON. Pardon me?

JOHN. For the work I do around the house. For being the student servant and taking care of the horses, taking care of the garden. I would like to be paid.

WILSON. Our agreement was that you would do it in exchange for your room and board.

JOHN. I understand that, sir.

WILSON. It's an even exchange, John.

JOHN. But I would still like to be paid. Even if it's an even exchange, I want to be paid for the work I do. I want to hold the money in my hand. I want to put the money in my pocket. Even if I give it right back to you after you give it to me, I still want to be paid.

WILSON. All right. I think I understand. Have you thought about how much you would like to be paid?

JOHN. You said it was an even exchange...

WILSON. All right, even exchange. How often would you like to be paid?

JOHN. How often do the men in the edifice pay for their room and board?

WILSON. Once a month.

JOHN. Then once a month. You pay me, I'll pay you.

WILSON. Okay, John. I think we can arrange that. Anything else?

JOHN. No, sir. Nothing else. Thank you. *(WILSON exits. JOHN speaks to audience.)* Over the next few months, I tried to figure out who had defaced that sign and written my name over that of Mongo the Ape's. Later, after I was invited to join the Athenian Literary Society, I got the opportunity to spend time with Mister Ward. He was the president of the society, which gave me ample opportunity to read his handwriting. This is where my suspicions about him turned into certainty.

(JANE enters with a shirt, hat, and pair of men's trousers.)

JANE. Here. This is for you.

JOHN. What?

JANE. New clothes. Not exactly new. New to you. Shirt, hat, trousers. They're cleaning you up. That's the first thing they do. They clean you up, then they get you fat. After that, ring the dinner bell 'cause it's suppertime. *(She offers him the clothes. He only looks at her.)* What you waiting for? Take it. Better than what you're wearing now. You ever wear a collared shirt before?

JOHN. No.

JANE. Better get used to it. It's going to be around your neck for a long time. It'll be your albatross.

JOHN. My what?

JANE. Albatross. From *The Rime of the Ancient Mariner* by Samuel Taylor Coleridge. Ever hear of it?

JOHN. No.

JANE. That's right, I forgot. You've taken up the Reverend's penchant for studying only dead men who wrote in Greek and Latin, and Coleridge is very much alive. He's English. But we won't hold that against him, now will we? He's a poet who wrote a poem about a sailor who kills a magical albatross that was trying to help him. For this crime against nature, the sailor was forced to wear the corpse of the bird around his neck.

Ah! well a-day! what evil looks
Had I from old and young!
Instead of the cross, the Albatross
About my neck was hung.

This collared shirt will be your albatross. Go ahead. Take it.

JOHN. If I have done something to disrespect you, I apologize.

JANE. Disrespect?

JOHN. All I've done since I've been here is try to please you. And all you've done in return is shown me contempt.

JANE. Perhaps my contempt stems from your incessant attempt to please. You ever think of that? You claim to be a free man of color, a man who is in control of his own destiny, but all I see you doing is running around here, nodding your head and smiling. And the type of head-nodding you're doing is not the type your father did. Now if that is who you are, all you have to do is say so, John. All you have to do is tell me that you don't want any trouble. Just tell me that the reason you're here is to make everybody happy and I will leave you alone, I swear, never again will you ever hear another cross word from me, butter won't melt in my mouth. But if you are the man you say you are, your desire to please makes my stomach turn.

JOHN. What's wrong with trying to please people?

JANE. Nothing. If that's the reason you're here. Is that the reason you're here? To dance for us, maybe sing a li'l song every now and then? To make everybody happy?

JOHN. I am here to be educated.

JANE. Educated? Such a big word for such a little boy.

JOHN. I have been chosen. Chosen to be governor of a new nation. Governor of a new world.

JANE. You say that as if it's something I didn't know. Is this news to you? I told you this when you first came here. They're training you. They're getting you ready. They're going to clean you up, get you fat, then prop you up in the window for the entire world to see. And you don't even give a damn. Like a hog gorging itself on slop, you don't care that the sound you hear in the background is that of a blade being sharpened. I have to admit, Robert knew what he was doing when he chose you. Here. Here's your clothes.

JOHN. I wasn't chosen by the Reverend. I was chosen by God.

JANE. 'Course you were. Here's your clothes. *(He takes the clothes.)* And I want to apologize. I apologize for everything I've said to you. I promise, you won't hear anything like that from me again. It's just that, when this moment came, I had hoped that somebody else would be standing where you're standing. But that's not your fault. You can't help who you are. You're just a poor ignorant beast being trained for something that you don't understand and I have to understand that that's not your fault. I'm sorry. I promise, I'll do better in the future. *(She exits. After a moment, JOHN starts to undress and eventually puts on the clothes.)*

JOHN *(to audience).* I had been called names before. Ignorant. Coon. Beast. Nigger. Of course, a colored man living in this country has seen hatred, sometimes on a daily basis. And any colored man living in this country who says that he has not been the object of hatred is either lying to you, or he hasn't been paying attention. So it was not the name-calling that bothered me. I think it was the pity with which she did it. While I had been, in the past, the object of hatred, I had never before been the object of naked pity. *(He has finished putting on the shirt, trousers and hat.)* Look at this. It fit. The trousers, the hat, the shirt, it all fit like it had been made for me. I had never worn a collared shirt before and expected the collar to be tight around my neck, but the shirt fit fine. In fact, the shirt was very comfortable. Except for one thing. It had an odor, a faint odor that I couldn't quite identify. After I tried on the shirt, the trousers and the hat, I sat in my room thinking about the pity that the wife of the Reverend had heaped upon me. Her pity became my pity and while I should have been very happy, the only thing I could think about was Mongo the Ape.

(Lights fade.)

END OF ACT ONE

ACT TWO

SCENE ONE

WILSON alone on stage as "Amazing Grace" plays in the background. WILSON appears to be uneasy. As the music plays, he keeps glancing offstage. Finally, the music comes to an end.

WILSON *(to audience).* Most distinguished guests, trustees, gentlemen... *(He stops, glances offstage.)* At this point in the program, I present to you John Newton Templeton. *(He glances offstage.)* The topic on which he will speak to you today is titled...is titled...

(JOHN enters. WILSON and JOHN exchange looks. WILSON exits.)

JOHN. The men of the American Colonization Society were an interesting bunch. While the organization claimed members from every state in the union, the ones who came to visit were from parts of Ohio, Pennsylvania, Virginia, the Carolinas, and Washington, D.C. Counting the good Reverend Wilson, there were twelve in all and as far as I could tell, all were pastors, preachers, ministers, and missionaries. Reverend Wilson had arranged this as the first of what was to be two meetings. It was scheduled during class hiatus so as not to interrupt my very important studies. The men arrived

49

throughout the day on a Monday and stayed for seven days. During those seven days, every morning I would recite for them, in either Latin or Greek, passages from Caesar's Commentaries, Cicero's Orations, and the Greek Testament. Afternoons were set aside for debate, or what they called debate. They gave me topics such as "Was the conspiracy against Julius Caesar justified?" Or "Should women be allowed to vote?" After stating the topic, they would then ask questions related to that topic and I would answer their questions. This was their idea of debate. We did this every afternoon from one until six. In the evenings, they had dinner during which they reviewed the events of the day. Being the student servant, I had the honor of serving them their dinner. During the first few days of this routine, I thought they were trying to see how smart I was, to see how much I knew. After a while, I realized that they were not trying to measure the depth and breadth of my knowledge. They were trying to determine if I was actually thinking for myself or if I was merely repeating what someone had taught me. When, on or about the fifth day, they realized that I was indeed thinking for myself, they seemed to be both delighted and surprised. Reverend Wilson was beaming like a proud new father and there I was in my shirt, trousers, and hat, performing for the gentlemen. For some reason, I couldn't get the image of Mongo out of my mind.

(JOHN sits and starts to read. WILSON enters.)

WILSON. You see what your president did?
JOHN. My president?

WILSON. John Quincy Adams.

JOHN. How did he become my president?

WILSON. If you could vote, you would have voted for him.

JOHN. But I didn't vote for him because I can't vote.

WILSON. But you would have. He would have been your choice. That makes him your president. You see what he did?

JOHN. What did he do?

WILSON. He appointed Henry Clay as Secretary of State.

JOHN. I heard about that.

WILSON. Which proves what I've been saying about the man all along. He is corrupt.

JOHN. Corrupt?

WILSON. Henry Clay ran against Adams for president. When it looked like Clay couldn't win, he had a meeting with Adams, withdrew his candidacy and then threw his support behind Adams. Adams gets elected and what does he do? He appoints Clay as Secretary of State.

JOHN. That's right. Clay helped him get elected. All Adams did was return the favor.

WILSON. Return the favor?

JOHN. I'd do it. If somebody helped me the way Clay helped Adams, I'd return the favor.

WILSON. Please don't tell me that. Please don't tell me that you would fall into the same trap.

JOHN. What trap?

WILSON. Adams didn't appoint Clay because he was the best man for the job. He didn't appoint him because he believed in what Clay stood for. Adams and Clay can't even agree on the color of the moon. The only reason Adams appointed Clay as Secretary of State was to uphold his end of a corrupt bargain. In Latin it's called quid pro quo. You know what that means?

JOHN. Yes.

WILSON. What?

JOHN. It means something given or received in exchange for something else.

WILSON. That's right. And when applied to politics, what does it imply?

JOHN. It implies a breach.

WILSON. What kind of a breach?

JOHN. A breach in the public trust.

WILSON. That's right. Now I hope you're not telling me that you would do the same. I hope you're not telling me that you would betray your own convictions in order to return a favor that someone did for you, because if so, we've made a terrible mistake.

JOHN. I suppose I would have to consider all of the ramifications.

WILSON. What's to consider? If someone asks you to betray your own convictions, you don't do it, John, no matter what that person did for you. Look at what I have here. *(He produces a letter.)* It's a letter from Reverend McLain. He talks about how impressed he and the other members of the committee were with your performance.

JOHN. My performance?

WILSON. On your oral examinations. Your performance exceeded everyone's expectations. They have asked me to officially ask you if you will accept their offer to become the first governor of Liberia.

JOHN. I thought we had to have an additional meeting.

WILSON. Apparently they didn't think it was necessary. You know why? Because they believe you to be a man of your convictions, John. They believe you to be a man who thinks for himself. A man who would not find himself in debt to some other man because of some small favor. I hope they're not mistaken. I hope that you are indeed a man of your convictions.

JOHN. I believe I am.

WILSON. I believe you are as well. I've written the committee and told them you've accepted their offer. In a couple of months, we ought to receive your official charter. Congratulations, Governor.

JOHN. When do I get to meet the others?

WILSON. The others?

JOHN. I'm going to have to establish a provisional government. I'm going to have to draft a political constitution and I'm going to have to establish a church. This is going to take years to accomplish and it's going to take more than just one man.

WILSON. Don't worry. We'll get you the help you need. Did you finish your essay for admission into the Literary Society?

JOHN. I finished.

WILSON. Did you give it to Mister Ward?

JOHN. I did.

WILSON. And?

JOHN. He rejected it.

WILSON. Rejected it?

JOHN. He said he wanted me to prepare a topic for debate instead.

WILSON. That Mister Ward is a rascal, isn't he?

JOHN. That would not be the term I would use.

WILSON. No need to be nasty, John. What topic for debate did they give you?

JOHN. "Why should ex-slaves go back to a land that sent them into slavery in the first place?"

WILSON. Interesting topic.

JOHN. Interesting?

WILSON. I'm sure you'll do just fine.

JOHN. He's baiting me.

WILSON. Probably.

JOHN. He heard about my meetings with the Colonization Society and he's baiting me.

WILSON. He's probably trying to test your mettle. That's all. See what you're made of.

JOHN. If he wants to see what I'm made of, all he has to do is read my essay. "The Claims of Liberia," that's what I'm made of. That's who I am. But he doesn't want to read it.

WILSON. The topic for debate is merely an exercise, John. An exercise in the powers of persuasion.

JOHN. I think they're looking for a reason not to admit me.

WILSON. Don't worry. You'll do fine. You know what today is? The first of the month. Time to settle our account. How's it going with the horses?

JOHN. Going fine.

WILSON. Jane tells me that the palomino looks a little lazy moving off her hind legs.

JOHN. She was dipping a bit under saddle, but her back right hoof needed a little trimming. I've already done it and she's moving just fine.

WILSON. Good work, John, thank you. How many hours do you have for the month?

JOHN. Let's see, three hours a day, six days a week, four weeks, that comes to seventy-two hours.

WILSON. Seventy-two hours at seven cents an hour...

JOHN. Five dollars and four cents.

WILSON *(pays JOHN)*. There you are.

JOHN. Thank you.

WILSON. Don't mention it. You earned every bit of it, Governor.

JOHN. I suppose I ought to settle up now as well.

WILSON. If you'd like.

JOHN. How much do I owe you?

WILSON. I'm not sure. Let's see, board is a dollar twenty-five a week.

JOHN. Four weeks.

WILSON. That comes to five dollars, even.

JOHN *(pays WILSON)*. There you are, sir.

WILSON. Thank you.

JOHN. My pleasure.

WILSON. Bet you never thought you'd come out ahead on the deal, did you?

JOHN. No, never thought that. By the way, I'll need a receipt.

WILSON. Pardon me?

JOHN. A receipt. For the money I paid you. I'll need a receipt.

WILSON. Yes. Of course. Let me just... *(WILSON writes out a receipt.)*

JOHN *(to audience)*. Holding true to your convictions may make your life more meaningful, but it was nothing like the thrill I got when payday rolled around and I got paid for the work I did. And then to pay for my own room and board, to pay my own way, to hold the receipts in my hand...

WILSON *(handing the receipt to JOHN)*. There you are.

JOHN. Thank you. *(WILSON exits. JOHN speaks to audience.)* I'll tell you, it was the sweetest honey, nothing
like it in the world. I prepared for my debate to enter
into the Literary Society. Or at least I tried to prepare.
"Why should ex-slaves go back to a land that sent them
into slavery in the first place?" I could answer the first
part of that question: Why should ex-slaves go back to
Africa? That part of the question, I had no problem with.
But why go back to a land that had sent them into slavery in the first place? Try as I might, I couldn't formu-
late a logical argument to that part of the question and
this bothered me. If I was going to go to Liberia, I
needed to be able to answer the second part of that question.

(JANE enters.)

JANE. I saw that Maybell was dipping a bit under saddle.
JOHN. She needed a little farrier work on her hind hooves.
I've already taken care of it.
JANE. You sure she didn't pull a muscle?
JOHN. Pretty sure.
JANE. If she pulled a muscle, she's going to need some at-
tention.
JOHN. You want me to take her out so you can inspect
her?
JANE. No, John, I trust you. I'm just concerned, that's all.
JOHN. I wouldn't let anything happen to that horse. I treat
her as if she were my own.
JANE. I know that. And I appreciate it. Thank you.
JOHN. No need to thank me. Just doing my job. Just doing
what I'm getting paid to do.

JANE. You know that she belongs to me.

JOHN. I know that, ma'am. It was just a figure of speech, that I treat her as if she were my own. I know she belongs to you.

JANE. No. I meant that Maybell used to be mine. Robert bought her when she was a filly and gave her to me as a present. He knew I always wanted a horse. He knew I wanted to learn to ride. Right after we moved here, my youngest boy, David, died and I guess he thought Maybell might lift my spirits a bit, which she did. Used to be my job to go out and groom her every day. Pulling, clipping, trimming. After a while, Reverend said I was paying too much attention to her. Said that if we left her out in the pasture where she could roll around on the ground, she wouldn't need to be groomed every day. But she liked it when I would come out and spend time with her. Seems like she knew when I was supposed to be there, and if I was late she'd let me know about it. If I was late, I'd see her hanging her head over the door. She'd see me and then start bumping the side of the stall with her hoof.

JOHN. She does that with me.

JANE. Seems like you can tell what she's thinking.

JOHN. She's a smart horse.

JANE. Yes, she is.

JOHN. How'd your boy die?

JANE. I had three boys. Matthew, Mark, and David. The oldest, Matthew, died of the cholera when he was eleven. Mark died of the yellow vomit when he was fourteen. And my baby, David, he lived to be nineteen years old. He wanted to be a preacher like his father. He wanted to prove to his father that he was good enough to march into the wilderness and spread the word of God. He thought that all you needed to go into the wilderness was the word of God. That armed with the word of God, the savages would fall to their knees and pray. But you need more than the word of God. You need to have a gun, and you need to have the heart to use it. But David didn't understand that. They found what was left of his body near what used to be a Shawnee encampment. Animals had gotten to it. And the Shawnee, they had stripped his body of everything they could use. Boots, belt, everything except his Bible.

JOHN. I'm sorry.

JANE. No need to be sorry. I'm done with my grieving. I have no more tears to shed.

JOHN. I'm taking Maybell into town. I'll make sure to pay attention to how she's riding. If anything's not right, I'll be sure to take care of it.

JANE. What you going into town for?

JOHN. Mister Morgan ordered some iron leg traps for me.

JANE. Iron leg traps?

JOHN. Deer got into the garden again. I figured if we can't scare them away, we'll trap 'em. Maybe have ourselves a little venison.

JANE. I don't want any iron leg traps in my garden.

JOHN. I'm not putting them in the garden. I'm going to put them in the deer run along the edge of the wood line.

JANE. Do you have to do it that way?

JOHN. Don't know of any other way. Hog's blood doesn't work.

JANE. It'll work.

JOHN. Didn't work over the last two springs. Didn't work over the summer.

JANE. Just can't use it all the time. First time deer smells blood, it scares 'em. Makes 'em think death is near. But if they smell old blood, they get used to it.

JOHN. You want me to go out there and sprinkle blood around the house and garden every day?

JANE. What you got to do is figure out when the herd is going to come, then spread the blood right before they get here. That way, it'll be fresh.

JOHN. How am I supposed to figure out when a herd of deer is going to come?

JANE. Used to be easy. They used to come every four to eight weeks. And there was a tribe of Miami that used to follow them. Small tribe. Peaceful. Maybe ten men. Twelve, maybe fifteen women. A brood of small children. You'd see them up on the north ridge. You'd see the Indians and know that the deer herd was somewhere near. But you don't see them anymore. Not around here.

JOHN. I saw some.

JANE. You saw some what?

JOHN. Indians. Three of them. Don't know what kind. Brave, squaw and a child. I was coming back from Albany. The lower plain was flooded so I was following the ridges on the way back. I had gotten lost, a little twisted around and that's when I rode up on the child, maybe three, four years old. He was just laying there, sleeping on a bed of pine needles. I got off the horse for a better look and that's when the brave appeared. I don't know who was more scared, me or him. Then the mother appeared, snatched up the baby and the three were gone, just like that.

JANE. You tell anybody?

JOHN. No.

JANE. Don't. Don't tell anyone.

JOHN. Why not?

JANE. They're probably Miami. They're peaceful. No need to say anything. Just keep it to yourself.

JOHN. You think the deer herd is near?

JANE. I don't know.

JOHN. You said they follow the herd.

JANE. I want you to figure out another way to keep the deer out.

JOHN. I don't know of any other way.

JANE. There's always another way.

JOHN. You said my job was to keep the deer out of the garden. If that's my job, you should let me do my job the best way I see fit.

JANE. All right. You're right. Make sure you keep the horses away. I don't want to see my Maybell get torn up by one of those devices.

JOHN. I'll keep her away.

JANE. Thank you, John.

JOHN *(moves to exit, stops)*. Ma'am?

JANE. Yes?

JOHN. Why don't you come out and ride with me one afternoon? I'll get Maybell ready and I'll take one of the other horses and we can go up around the north ridge if you want. It's real pretty this time of the year. Or if you want, I'll get Maybell ready and you can just go off on your own. Whatever you prefer.

JANE. Whatever I prefer. You know what I would prefer? I would prefer that you did just that. I would prefer that you went out right now and put a saddle on Maybell and

I would get on her and I would ride her into town. I would prefer to get on her and ride her to someplace far away from here. But that's not going to happen, is it?

JOHN. I could get her ready if you want.

JANE. Are you trying to be mean to me or are you just stupid?

JOHN. Ma'am?

JANE. I've been treating you with a civil tongue and would prefer if you did the same.

JOHN. I'm not trying to be mean to you.

JANE. Then you're just stupid.

JOHN. I'm sorry if I said something to offend you.

JANE. Men ride horses, John.

JOHN. What do you mean?

JANE. Men ride horses and I am not a man.

JOHN. I've seen women ride horses.

JANE. Sidesaddle. But you can't climb a hill sidesaddle. You can't ford a stream sidesaddle.

JOHN. What about the women in the town? Miss Clark? Miss Thompson? And the women in the circus. They don't ride sidesaddle.

JANE. Miss Clark, Miss Thompson and the women in the circus are not considered to be women. They look like women. They got the parts of a woman but they smoke tobacco. They spit. They're unmarried. They have no home, they have no God. These are not women, John. They're freaks. Aberrations. Abominations.

JOHN. Abominations?

JANE. A woman would never ride with her legs splayed open astride a beast, and I am a woman. I'm not supposed to ride with my legs splayed open. I have to ride in the buckboard or in a wagon. I have to have a man drive me to any place I want to go. But you, you can ride. An ex-slave gets on my horse and rides but I can't ride. I'm not allowed. I'm not allowed because I'm a woman.

JOHN. I didn't know that.

JANE. What do you know other than Latin and Greek?

JOHN. I'm sorry.

JANE. Nothing in the Bible says a woman can't ride a horse. At least, I don't think there is, but I don't know for sure 'cause I can't read Hebrew. Least, I can't read it well enough to tell. And the English Bible, the King James Bible, they say that's not God's word. They say it's what King James said the Bible says. So until I learn how to read Hebrew, I won't know whether the Bible is against it or not.

JOHN. Would you like to learn?

JANE. Learn what?

JOHN. Learn how to read Hebrew.

JANE. You going to teach me?

JOHN. I could.

JANE. That's very sweet of you.

JOHN. I could do it.

JANE. You think that would change things? You think teaching me how to read Hebrew or teaching me how to read Greek is going to stop this awful, hateful thing from growing inside of me? They brought you here and they let you go to school but they won't let me go to school. My husband is president of the university and I can't even step foot inside the door. Not unless I'm looking to do laundry. Wash the sheets. Clean the floors. Every time I found out I was going to have a child, I would pray to God and ask God to please God please don't let it be a girl. I would rather it be born dead and I'd feed it to the hogs than it be born a girl. 'Cause I wouldn't know how to explain to a girl that the hunger she had inside would never be satisfied. I wouldn't know how to teach a girl to never look to the stars but to keep her head bowed down in subservient submission to some man. So I asked God to please God give me boys and God answered my prayers. One by one, he gave me three beautiful healthy boys. And then, one by one, he took those boys away. I grieved for them, one by one and then I stopped grieving. Then you came. You could teach me how to read Hebrew and you could teach me how to read Greek, but that isn't going to change anything. I still can't step foot inside the door. I am still forced to stand here and watch while they let you in over me. They let you in. They welcome you with open arms. They give you this gift and what do you do? You squander it.

JOHN. I'm sorry you feel that way.

JANE. Why you sorry? If you're going to be a houseboy for the slave owners of this world, don't be sorry about it. Stand up and be proud that you're their houseboy.

JOHN. I'm nobody's houseboy.

JANE. You go to Liberia, you're going to be the houseboy for every man that has ever bought, sold or traded in human flesh in this world. "Yes sir, Master, you got some niggers you done using? Ah'll take ker of 'em fer ya."

JOHN. Sometimes the limitations of your comprehension are downright embarrassing.

JANE. The limitations of my comprehension?

JOHN. I am truly sorry that you feel the way you do. However, ultimately, what you think, how you feel, your opinion on what I'm about to do is of absolutely no consequence to me. You want me to stand up for what I believe in? I am standing. You want me to be proud of the choice I've made? I am proud, I am happy and I am humbled to be able to carry out the will of our Lord God Jesus Christ.

JANE. Typical nigger. Don't know the difference between the will of God and the will of a slave owner.

JOHN. I don't know any slave owners. The only slave owner I know died a long time ago.

JANE. Who do you think is running the ACS? They're slave owners, John. All of them. They all either own slaves now or did own slaves at one point in their lives. That's their bond-ship. That's the thing that binds them together. And you're too stupid to see that you're doing exactly what they want you to do. You go to Liberia and take all of the free men of color with you, who will that leave here in this country? Only the slaves, John. Only the slaves. And what will happen if they ever let a woman get anything other than an elementary school education? Will she have to leave the country as well? Is that the price we have to pay for challenging what they believe, for challenging their dogma? Banishment? I can't go to school. I can't ride a horse. Maybell is my horse. Reverend gave her to me. He said she was mine. But all I can do is look at her. All I can do is stand there and watch while somebody else rides. They're giving you your own country. Will you be able to ride? *(JANE exits.)*

JOHN *(to audience)*. The Indians I saw, I saw as I was on my way back from Albany. I had ridden out there because I heard rumors about a free man who had opened a school and since it was only about ten, twelve miles out, I wanted to go see for myself. The man's name was Jonathan Goodman and when I got there, all I saw was one room which also served as his living quarters. In that room he had three books. One Bible, the English King James version, a very elementary book on world geography, and a book called *The Life of Gustavus Vassa, the African*. There was not one volume of Latin verses, not one volume of Greek philosophy, and after talking to him, I found out that he didn't even have any students. Hardly the ingredients of what I would call a school. I asked him, I said, "Where are the students?" Poor man, he looked around the empty room and said, "They are here. They're here." Not wanting to embarrass him by leaving straight away, I picked up *The Life of Gustavus Vassa* and started to page through it. I found out that Gustavus had been a slave in Africa before being sold to an American slave trader. But his description of what he called African slavery bore no resemblance to the institution we had come to know in America. While he was certainly owned while in Africa, the African sense of ownership was different than ours. Gustavus seemed to be owned by the entire community and he had a place in that community. He was never required to do any more work than the other members of the community, he was allowed to own his own property, and he was allowed to have a family and that family was kept intact. There was none of the cruelty and inhumanity that permeated American slavery. In fact, the only similarity between African slavery and American slavery was that they were both, for some reason, called slavery. This was not what I had been led to believe about Africa. "Why should ex-slaves go back to a land that was the birthplace of slavery?" Because Africa was not the birthplace of slavery. At least not the type of slavery that had a stranglehold on America. I thought this was the answer. The answer to the only question I had left. Until I realized that I would soon be there in Africa. That I would soon hear all of these different languages and see for myself all of these strange customs. I realized that these were the people that I had been chosen to bring civilization to. That's when I started to have my first real doubts because from what I read during those couple of hours, it didn't appear as if these people were the ones who needed the civilization.

(WILSON enters with a leather bag containing a flint-lock pistol, powder, ball bag, and horn, all of which he starts to unpack.)

WILSON. John? How about after supper you get the horses ready and you and I go out riding. I want to look around down near the river.

JOHN. Sounds good to me.

WILSON. And I heard back from Reverend McLain. He's found a man he wants you to meet. Another free man of color who could assist you in Liberia. Reverend McLain is going to bring him when he comes for your graduation. You can meet this man, talk to him, and if you like him, he can stay here and begin his training in the fall.

JOHN. Don't you mean his education?

WILSON. I'm sorry?

JOHN. You said he can begin his training in the fall. I think you meant to say his education.

WILSON. Training, education. Same thing.

JOHN. Not quite. Training comes from the Latin, traginare, meaning to draw out and manipulate in order to bring about a desired form. When you train something, you manipulate it to follow, to come after or behind. But the word educate, it comes from the Latin, educare, meaning to develop the power of reasoning and judgment. Manipulate to follow, come after or behind. Autonomy, power, reasoning, and judgment. Two words. Two very different meanings.

WILSON. My my, aren't we the scholar?

JOHN. Just pointing out the difference. That's all.

WILSON. All right. He can come for your graduation and if you like him, he can begin his education in the fall. Is that better?

JOHN. Thank you.

WILSON. And that essay you wrote for Mister Ward? "The Claims of Liberia?" I want you to use that as your graduation speech.

JOHN. I had thought about doing a Latin oration.

WILSON. Latin oration?

JOHN. Something from Plato's "Symposium."

WILSON. All of your classmates will be doing Latin orations, John.

JOHN. That's the reason I would like to do one.

WILSON. There's nothing special about a Latin oration. And the trustees are already questioning the value of a liberal arts education. We need to show them that we're doing more than simply studying Latin and Greek. We need to show them that we are actively engaged in shaping the face of America, engaged in shaping the future of the world. "The Claims of Liberia" will do that for us. Forget about doing a Latin oration. I think nine Latin orations will be quite enough, thank you. You ever load and fire a Kentucky flintlock pistol before?

JOHN. No sir.

WILSON. You ever load and fire any type of pistol before?

JOHN. No.

WILSON. You must always remember to make sure that the ball is seated firmly up against the powder charge. If you try to fire with the ball off the charge, the thing'll blow up in your face. Here, look at this. She's a beauty, isn't she? *(He hands the pistol to JOHN.)* First thing you do is check to make sure the barrel is clear. Go ahead. Check.

JOHN. You want me to carry a pistol to the next meeting of the Literary Society?

WILSON. Why would I want you to do something like that?

JOHN. Because of Mister Ward.

WILSON. Mister Ward?

JOHN. He fired a pistol at Mister McCoy. During debate. I thought you knew.

WILSON. No.

JOHN. They were debating the merits of religious devotion and Mister Ward was losing the debate. When somebody started to laugh, Mister Ward pulled out a pistol and fired it at Mister McCoy. Mister McCoy fell to the floor. We all thought he was dead.

WILSON. Was he hit?

JOHN. He fainted. Which of course meant that Mister Ward won the debate.

WILSON. Nobody told me anything about this.

JOHN. I thought that was the reason...

WILSON. Somebody spotted some Indians not far from here. That's the reason for the pistol.

JOHN. Indians?

WILSON. Every now and then you come across a couple of stragglers. That's what these probably are. Stragglers living in the caves in the outlying regions. Nothing to worry about. The government's going to send out some riders to track them down. They'll find them, relocate them. Send them to live with the rest of their people.

JOHN. If there's nothing to worry about, why do you need a pistol?

WILSON. You never can be too safe. Besides, you're going to need to know how to fire a pistol once you get to Liberia. Now, check to make sure that the barrel is clear. Once you're sure that the barrel is clear, you add your powder charge.

JOHN. What do I do about the people who are already there?

WILSON. Already where? What people?

JOHN. In Liberia. When I get there, what do I do about the people already there?

WILSON. It's a wilderness, John. There are no people there.

JOHN. Natives. What do I do about the natives?

WILSON. That's up to you. You offer them the word and if they refuse that word... *(Beat.)*

JOHN. If they refuse?

WILSON. I suggest that you give them the option of determining their own fate. If they refuse the word then one option would be to relocate them. Not you, personally, of course. You'll have men to do that for you. Now check your barrel. Make sure it's clear.

JOHN. Where does it stop?

WILSON. Where does what stop?

JOHN. I relocate the people who are there, they relocate someone else. Where does it stop?

WILSON. Relocation is only an option, John. They don't have to be relocated. They can accept the gift of civilization.

JOHN. I'm not quite sure it's a gift.

WILSON. What're you talking about?

JOHN. We seem to be caught in this vicious circle. The English came to Ireland, the Irish came to America, now you're sending me to Liberia. Where do the Liberians go?

WILSON. I'm sure you'll be able to find a place for them.

JOHN. The way Andrew Jackson found a place for the Shawnee?

WILSON. Are you trying to be insolent?

JOHN. I don't think I'm the right man for this.

WILSON. 'Course you are, John.

JOHN. I feel like I'm giving up without even trying. You said your father fought against the English. But he fought. He didn't give up when somebody asked him to move. He fought, he struggled, he tried to keep his home before striking out to find a new home. And even then, he didn't abandon that fight until after it became clear that he couldn't win that fight. Here I am, I haven't even tried.

WILSON. Tried what?

JOHN. Tried to make this my home. I've given up without even trying.

WILSON. But this is not your home, John. Your home is in Africa.

JOHN. My home is here in the United States.

WILSON. But your people are from Africa.

JOHN. And your people are from Ireland but I don't see you getting on a boat to go back. My family has been in this country for six generations. Five generations longer than your family. My father cut and fitted by hand every single piece of wood in the main library of the White House. But yet, you tell me that I'm the one who has to go? No, I'm sorry, but I can't do it, I won't do it. Not without first trying to make this my home.

WILSON. This will never be your home. Your people will never be able to live in harmony with the white race here in America. And this was not my doing, this was God's design. God made your people black, not me. And unless you can figure out a way to change your color, you will never be able to integrate into this society.

JOHN. You talk as if it's already been determined.

WILSON. It has been determined. Determined by God. God brought your people here as slaves, as savages. Now God has opened the way for you to return to Africa laden with the fruits of civilization.

JOHN. God did not bring my people here.

WILSON. God opened the way.

JOHN. Slave traders brought my people here.

WILSON. They were the instruments guided by the hand of God.

JOHN. Are you saying that slavery was part of God's design?

WILSON. I am saying that everything in this world is part of God's design. We may not always understand the reasons why God does what he does, but if we have faith and do not question his word, in time, he will reveal the truth and he will reveal the way. Now, I'm going to try to forget everything you just said. I'm going to try to forgive you but I never want to hear anything like that from you again. You're nervous. I understand that. You have concerns. But you're also educated, John. You should know better. Now, you know what today is? First of the month. Time to settle our accounts. How many hours do you have for the month? *(Beat.)* John? How many hours?

JOHN. Seventy-two.

WILSON. Same as always. Seventy-two hours at seven cents an hour. That's five dollars and four cents for the month. *(WILSON pays JOHN.)* There you are.

JOHN. Thank you.

WILSON. Don't mention it. You earned every bit of it. Governor.

JOHN. I have work to do. *(JOHN moves to exit.)*

WILSON. John? *(JOHN stops.)* Aren't you forgetting something? Don't you think you should settle your account as well?

JOHN. Who founded the ACS?

WILSON. Pardon me?

JOHN. I want to know who founded the ACS.

WILSON. You know who founded the ACS.

JOHN. Tell me again.

WILSON. You know them. You met them. Many of them. Reverend Jacobs. Reverend McLain.

JOHN. Who else?

WILSON. Andrew Jackson.

JOHN. Andrew Jackson.

WILSON. Francis Scott Key.

JOHN. Slave owners.

WILSON. Maybe, at one point in their lives.

JOHN. What about you?

WILSON. What about me?

JOHN. Are you a former slave owner?

WILSON. What I used to do or who I used to be is none of your concern.

JOHN. Only by studying the origins of a thing—

WILSON. Language, John. I was talking about language.

JOHN. But language is not the end. Our goal is not to understand the words. Our goal is to understand all of the things the words represent, and if I am being asked to leave my country, to leave the land of my birth, I have the right to know who's doing the asking.

WILSON. God is doing the asking.

JOHN. Slave owners and former slave owners are doing the asking.

WILSON. You're named after a slave owner. Did you know that? You're named after John Newton who bought and sold hundreds of slaves. But he received second sight. God allowed him to see the wickedness of his ways and then God inspired him to write a song of praise about it. "Amazing Grace." You ever hear it? *(He sings.)*

> Amazing grace, how sweet the sound,
> That saved a wretch like me,
> I once was lost, but now am found,
> Was blind but now I see.

You should be grateful for former slave owners because they are the only friends you have. The abolitionists are not your friends. The only thing the abolitionists are doing is exacerbating the problem. But the former slave owners have seen the problem firsthand, they have sat at the table and dined with misery, they have had intercourse with suffering, they have conducted commerce with the devil himself and now they have second sight. They see a world that they've never seen before and that world looks different, John. Like the morning you were born. The entire world looks different.

JOHN. A world that looks white. Is that how they see the world with their second sight? A white world cleansed of all of their sins? Is that the reason they want to ship all of the niggers back to Africa? So that they won't have to be reminded of their sins?

WILSON. How dare you speak to me that way.

JOHN. I won't do it, Reverend. I refuse to take a part in the whitewashing of this country.

WILSON. You don't have any choice in the matter.

JOHN. I've always had a choice.

WILSON. You never had a choice. Never. From the day you were born, this was your destiny. This is the reason God saved you. This is what God has chosen you for.

JOHN. Then why doesn't God tell me that? Why doesn't God speak to me and tell me this?

WILSON. Have you been listening? Have you been open to receive the word of God?

JOHN. I've been listening all right. But the only voice I hear is a voice telling me that if I go to Liberia, the only thing I will do is contribute to more bloodshed and more death.

WILSON. Bloodshed and death are parts of life, John. Life is blood and there could be no life without death. Civilization grinds on. Men who refuse to be a part of civilization's progress are crushed under her slow-moving weight. You try to back out of this now and you will be crushed. I will not let you graduate, the entire time you spent here will be wasted and you will leave here as a failure. Your failure will confirm many people's suspicions that your people don't have the discipline, nor the intelligence for higher education. You back out of this now and you will be the last free man of color to attend university here or anywhere else in this country, I guarantee it. There are a lot of eyes upon you, John. And you've been doing well. Don't falter. Now, I think it's time to settle your account.

JOHN. I'll settle my account when I get ready. *(JOHN exits.)*

SCENE TWO

JANE on stage. JOHN enters.

JANE. You find it?

JOHN. I found it.

JANE. What was it?

JOHN. I don't know.

JANE. You don't know?

JOHN. By the time I got there, there was nothing left. Nothing but blood. Pieces of bone. Small pieces of flesh.

JANE. The coyotes got to it.

JOHN. I didn't see any coyotes.

JANE. I saw them. They were feeding on it.

JOHN. I didn't see any coyotes.

JANE. That's because by the time you got there, there was no reason for them to still be there. There was nothing left. Something got caught in that iron leg trap of yours and the coyotes got to it. They killed it. They ripped it apart.

JOHN. It was probably just a deer.

JANE. Wasn't a deer.

JOHN. How do you know?

JANE. I saw it. It was too small to be a deer.

JOHN. Then a fox. It was probably a fox.

JANE. I told you to be careful where you put those iron leg traps.

JOHN. It was just a fox. That's all it was. There's nothing to worry about. I'll go out and collect up the rest of the traps. Give them back to Mister Morgan. *(JOHN moves to exit.)*

JANE. John? Robert says you've changed your mind about going to Liberia.

JOHN. That's right.

JANE. He also said you plan to give a Latin oration for graduation.

JOHN. If I'm not going to Liberia, I shouldn't give a speech supporting the idea, should I?

JANE. John...

JOHN. I guess I should thank you.

JANE. Don't thank me.

JOHN. But you were right, Missus Wilson.

JANE. No, John.

JOHN. You were right about everything.

JANE. The only thing I was concerned about was myself, John. I shouldn't have spoken to you the way I did.

JOHN. I was being trained for something I didn't understand.

JANE. I want you to give your "Claims of Liberia" speech.

JOHN. Why?

JANE. Robert won't tell you this, but the university is in trouble. Financially. The people in town can't pay the money they owe and we were depending upon that money to stay open but there is no money. And the trustees, the trustees won't release any more money until they have had a look at the graduating class. They want evidence that the work Robert is doing here has an impact on the world outside. I'm not asking you to go to Liberia, John. But I am asking you to give your speech. "The Claims of Liberia" will be the evidence Robert needs to prove that the work he's doing here is important. But if you give a Latin oration, all the trustees will see will be more of the same of what they've seen in the past. They will not give us the money we need and the university will close.

JOHN. You're asking me to enter into a corrupt bargain.

JANE. You really don't believe that, do you?

JOHN. I don't believe you're asking me to do this.

JANE. I'm asking you to help a man who has treated you like a son.

JOHN. A son?

JANE. He brought you into this house, he protected you. I see the way he looks at you, the way he treats you, he doesn't treat any of the other students that way.

JOHN. False words are not only evil in themselves, but they inflict the soul with evil. That's what you're asking me to do. You're asking me to inflict my soul with evil.

JANE. Is that the only thing you're concerned about? Yourself? Your soul?

JOHN. If I don't look after my soul, no one else will.

JANE. You know what an ape is? An ape is a beast that lives a solitary existence aware of only one thing. Its own needs, itself in the present. That's what you are. A goddamn ape. Oblivious to everything except yourself.

JOHN. I may have been an ape once but not anymore. Here. Here's your shirt. *(He takes the shirt off, throws it at her.)* Stinking ape shirt. Smell of that shirt made me sick. Reminded me of everything I was doing. I'd wash it and wash it but the smell of that shirt wouldn't come out.

JANE. This shirt used to belong to my baby boy, David. Robert tried to make me give you this shirt, but I wouldn't do it. He said I was suffering from female hysteria but still, I wouldn't do it. Then he took you out riding. The only other person he would go riding with was David. I remember one afternoon looking out the window and seeing you two on horseback, hearing your voices, you riding alongside Robert and for a moment, I thought that my son had come home. That's when I realized why he wanted me to give you the shirt. So I gave you David's shirt, his hat, his pants. *(She smells the shirt.)* And that smell is David's smell. His sweat. God how I used to love that smell. *(She smells the shirt.)* Only now, his smell has gotten all mixed up with your smell and I don't know whether to embrace it or fall away in utter revulsion.

(WILSON enters.)

WILSON. They found the Indians. They were Miami. They had to kill the brave.

JOHN. What do you mean they had to kill him?

WILSON. He was a savage, John.

JOHN. But why did they have to kill him?

WILSON. He came out of the woods and charged us. He was on foot and tried to attack six men on horseback. One of the men in the party, he spoke Algonquian. He shouted, "We're not here to hurt you. We want to help you." But the brave, he had a knife. He kept cutting and slashing. If they hadn't killed him, he would have certainly injured or killed one of us.

JOHN. What about the woman?

WILSON. We found her sitting at the foot of an oak tree. We rode up on her and she just sat there. She didn't try to run. She didn't try to fight. She just sat there, staring out, covered with blood. Looked like she had been attacked. Bitten. Probably coyote. She had bites on her arms, her hands. Looks like she had to fight them off.

JOHN. And the child?

WILSON. What child?

JOHN. There was a child. Three, four years old.

WILSON. There was no child.

JOHN. A little boy. I saw him.

WILSON. There was no child. We looked, but there was no child to be found. We found the brave and found the squaw. If there was a child don't you think we would have found him as well?

JANE. Told you it wasn't a fox. God, it wasn't a fox.

JOHN. What are they going to do with the woman?

WILSON. Send her to live with the rest of her people. She'll be happier there. This is your pistol, John. I bought it for you. I was going to teach you how to use it, then give it to you as a gift for graduation. I made that mistake once. You want it?

JOHN. No.

WILSON. You're going to need it, John. Where's your shirt?

JANE. Here.

WILSON. It's midday, man. Why aren't you wearing it? *(Beat.)* Put it on.

JOHN. No.

WILSON. No?

JOHN. I'm not wearing it anymore.

WILSON. Would somebody please explain to me where I went wrong with you. *(No one answers.)* The trustees are going to be here in two weeks. I need to start putting together a program for commencement. Would you like to be included in that program? Have you decided what you're going to do?

JOHN. I told you what I was going to do.

WILSON. Tell me again.

JOHN. You're going to have to find somebody else to go to Liberia.

WILSON. You're turning your back on God?

JOHN. Your God, maybe, but not my God.

WILSON. There's only one God, John.

JOHN. I think I read the Bible a bit differently than you do.

WILSON. And there's only one way to read the Bible.

JOHN. Your God brought slaves here in chains. My God wept while it was happening.

WILSON. That's blasphemy. Not only do you turn your back on God but you blaspheme while doing it? I think you should collect your things, John. It's time for you to leave this house.

JOHN. And go where?

WILSON. That's up to you. You have your papers, I imagine you can travel any place in the state you please, but you have to leave here. The university. The town.

JOHN. What about graduation?

WILSON. You're not graduating.

JANE. You can't do that, Robert.

JOHN. I've completed all of the requirements for graduation.

JANE. You can't do this.

WILSON. If he doesn't go to Liberia, if he fails to recognize the overwhelming facts pointing to him being the one chosen to do this, then he has failed in his education.

JOHN. My education or my training?

WILSON. Your education.

JOHN. I still don't think you understand the difference between the two.

WILSON. And you have no idea of what's at stake here. You want to prove that you're as good as white? Stand up and embrace your destiny, John. You have to become a leader. That's the reason I brought you here, that's what the trustees want to see. They allowed me to bring you here and now they want to see a man who is on his way to becoming a leader.

JOHN. If I'm going to be a leader I need to do it how I see fit. Not in the way you think I should. My people don't need to wander through the wilderness to find a new home, they've already been on a journey, and that journey was to come here. Now if you set out to train me, you're right, I have failed in that training, you were unsuccessful in teaching me how to blindly follow orders, I do not sit up and speak on command. But if your goal was to educate me, then I would like to congratulate you, because you did a very good job. You taught me how to think for myself, you taught me about a world I didn't even know existed. But if that was your goal, if your goal was to educate me, then you must now give me the freedom to come to my own conclusions.

JANE. He's right, Robert. You have to let him go.

WILSON. No.

JANE. Let him go, Robert.

WILSON. God sent him here for me. God took away my sons then He gave me John. Don't you see? You are mine, John. God gave you to me. You belong to me.

JANE. He doesn't belong to you, Robert.

WILSON. God gave him to me.

JANE. He doesn't belong to anyone.

JOHN. Here. This is the five dollars I owe you for the last month's room and board. Thank you for taking me in. I'll get my things.

JANE. Wait, John, no. You don't have to go. You can stay here. Robert? Tell him he doesn't have to go. Robert?

WILSON. Five dollars? After everything I gave you, this is what you give me in return? Five goddamn dollars?

JOHN. If you want me to give "The Claims of Liberia" speech, I'll do it. You know why? Because I have carefully considered and come to the conclusion that it's the right thing to do. You're right, you have done a lot for me and I would like to return the favor so I'll give the speech. But don't ask me to go to Liberia. If it means I won't graduate, if it means I have to leave this house today, then I'll leave. But I'm not going to Liberia, Reverend. I'm not going to do it.

WILSON. I'll add your name to the program. *(WILSON exits.)*

JANE. John? Would you like to have your shirt back?

JOHN. Thank you. *(She hands him the shirt, then exits. JOHN speaks to audience.)* I gave the speech, but never did go to Liberia. And I did graduate with nine other men. We all received diplomas which were, by the way, at the time, real sheepskin.

After graduation I moved around a bit and eventually ended up in Wheeling, Virginia, now called West Virginia, where I started a school. I had a little money. I had saved four cents a month for almost four years. That gave me exactly one dollar and twenty-two cents which I used to purchase three books for my new school. I purchased an English King James version of the Bible, an elementary book on world geography, and a copy of *The Life of Gustavus Vassa, the African*. Two weeks after opening my school, I was arrested and jailed for teaching colored folks how to read. But that didn't stop me. I taught in parts of Ohio, Virginia, and Pennsylvania.

And I was not the last free man of color to go to school at Ohio University. Four years after I graduated, Edward Roye was admitted. I imagine that his life here was much like mine, except for one small difference. He eventually became president of Liberia where he reigned for a year and a half, until the day that the captain of his army walked into his office and arrested him on charges of embezzlement. Corruption. So it began.

For a long time I was worried about my soul. I worried that I had failed to live up to God's plan, that I had failed to fulfill my destiny. But I now realize I didn't have to go to Liberia to start a new life, to work my way through the wilderness, to discover a new frontier. I had worked my way through the wilderness and had discovered a new frontier and that new frontier was inside of me.

(WILSON enters.)

WILSON. Ladies and gentlemen, most distinguished assembled guests, at this point in the program, I present to you John Newton Templeton.

(Lights fade.)

END OF PLAY

DIRECTOR'S NOTES

DIRECTOR'S NOTES

DIRECTOR'S NOTES

DIRECTOR'S NOTES